# A TO Z
# THE REAL DC

## by the tutors of
## Reach Incorporated

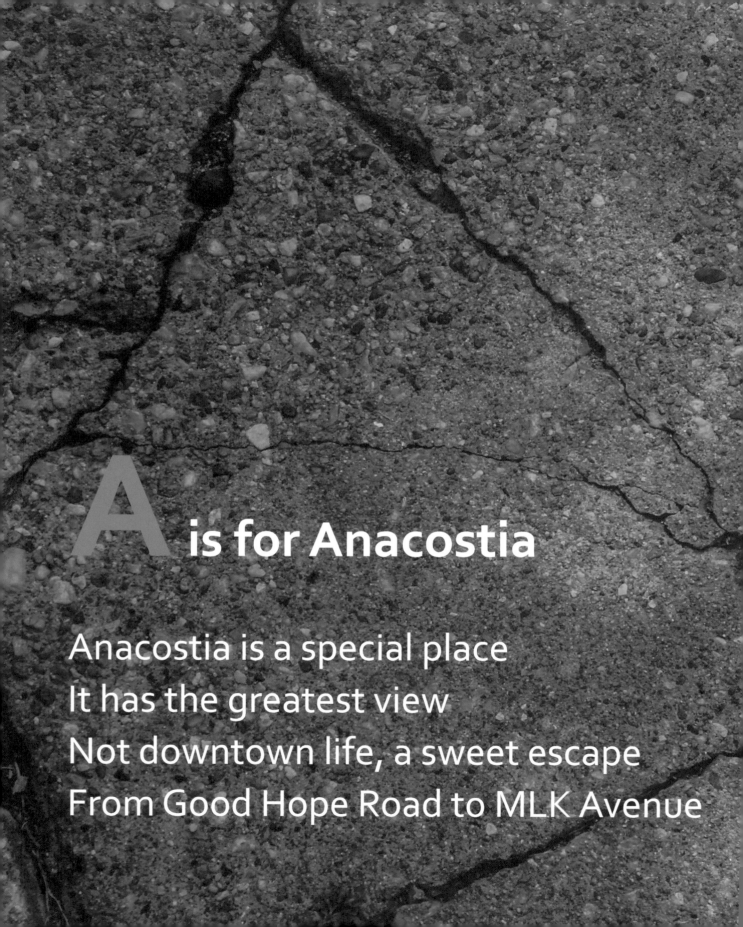

# A is for Anacostia

Anacostia is a special place
It has the greatest view
Not downtown life, a sweet escape
From Good Hope Road to MLK Avenue

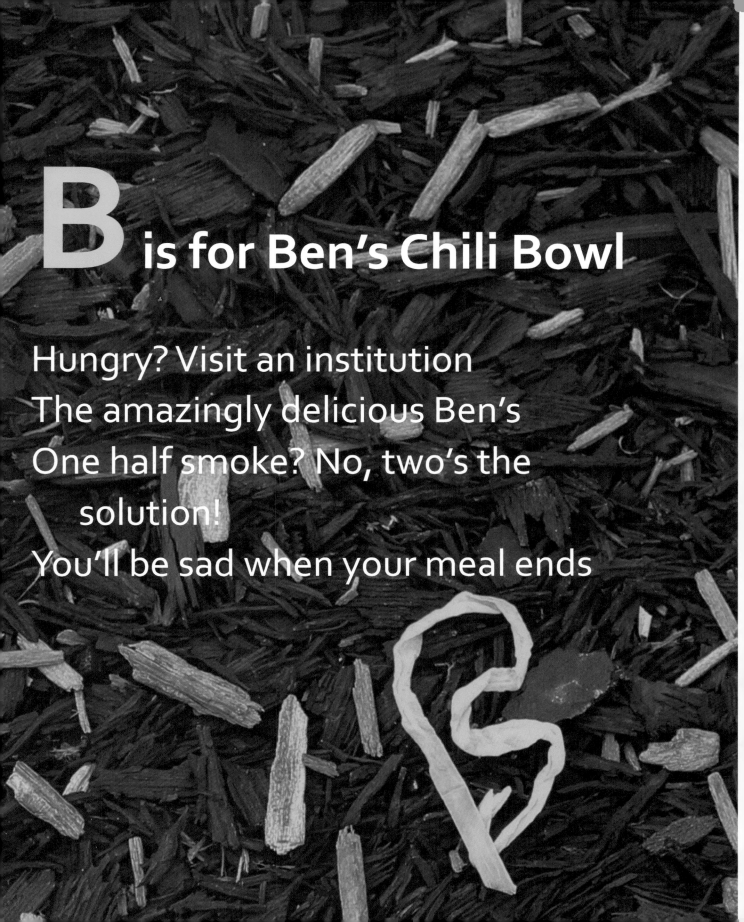

# B is for Ben's Chili Bowl

Hungry? Visit an institution
The amazingly delicious Ben's
One half smoke? No, two's the
    solution!
You'll be sad when your meal ends

# C is for Carry Out

The Carry Out is where you get
   tasty things
When you're so hungry your tummy
   aches
Order mumbo sauce on your fries
   and wings
It may take a while, but it's worth
   the wait

# D is for Duke Ellington

Jazz is smooth like a baby's tail
Telling a story in sounds so smart
Always hot and never stale.
Duke was DC's king. Now, a school
of art

# E

## is for Eastern Market

Have a weekend morning with
 nothing to do?
Eastern Market is good for eats
There are lots of vendors and a flea
 market too
At Seventh and C Southeast

# F is for Frederick Douglass

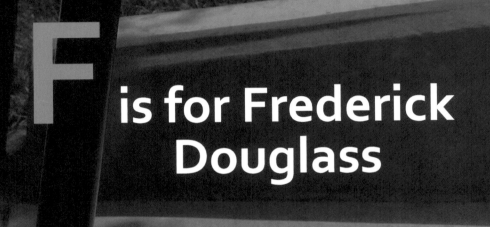

Frederick Douglass lived east of the
   river
On his Anacostia estate
The speeches that he delivered
Changed the black man's fate

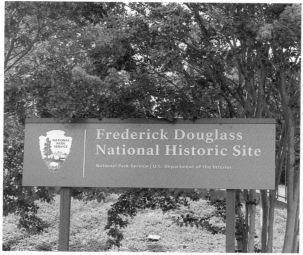

# G is for Go-Go

It all started with a man named Chuck
Drummers drum and hype men shout
To the beat, we dive and duck
In DC, Go-Go's what it's all about

# H

## is for Howard University

A local college, good ol' H U
Teachers teach and students learn
You can play, but study hard too
So a good job is what you'll earn

# I is for Icy Treats

Icy treats on a hot, hot day
Sweetness in the summer sun
Let's go to the pool and play
Wait!  It's the ice cream truck...RUN!

# J is for Justice

DC is the Supreme Court's home
And where Congress passes laws
Casting votes under the Capitol dome
All for justice's cause

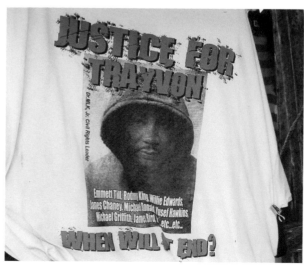

# K is for Kenilworth Aquatic Gardens

In a marsh, where songbirds fly
Lilies and lotuses, rare and pretty
A perfect collection of sea, land,
   and sky
In Kenilworth, right here in our city

# L is for Library of Congress

The Library of Congress on Capitol Hill
Has every book you'll ever need
It's the world's biggest library and
growing still
We hope you like to read!

# M is for Monuments and Memorials

Lincoln, Jefferson, and Dr. King
Be sure you see them all
The city fills up every single spring
When people visit the National Mall

# N is for Nationals Park

Nationals Park is home to our baseball
  stars
Hot dogs!  Peanuts!  The stadium's
  loud
Take the Green Line, it's not too far
Just follow the sound of the crowd

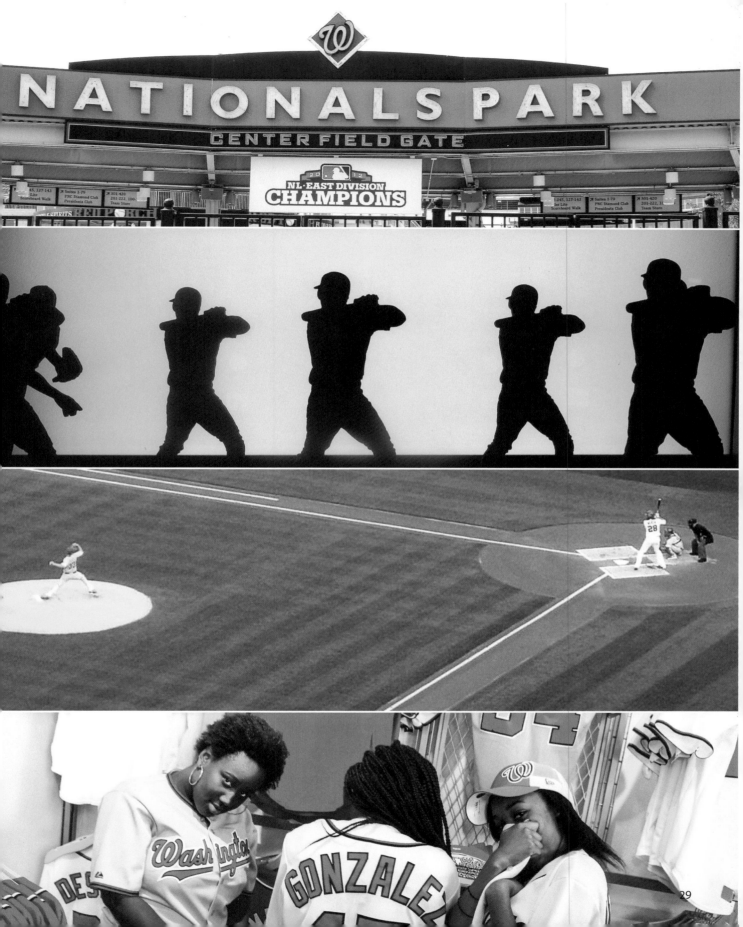

29

BARACK
OBAMA

44th
President

HOPE

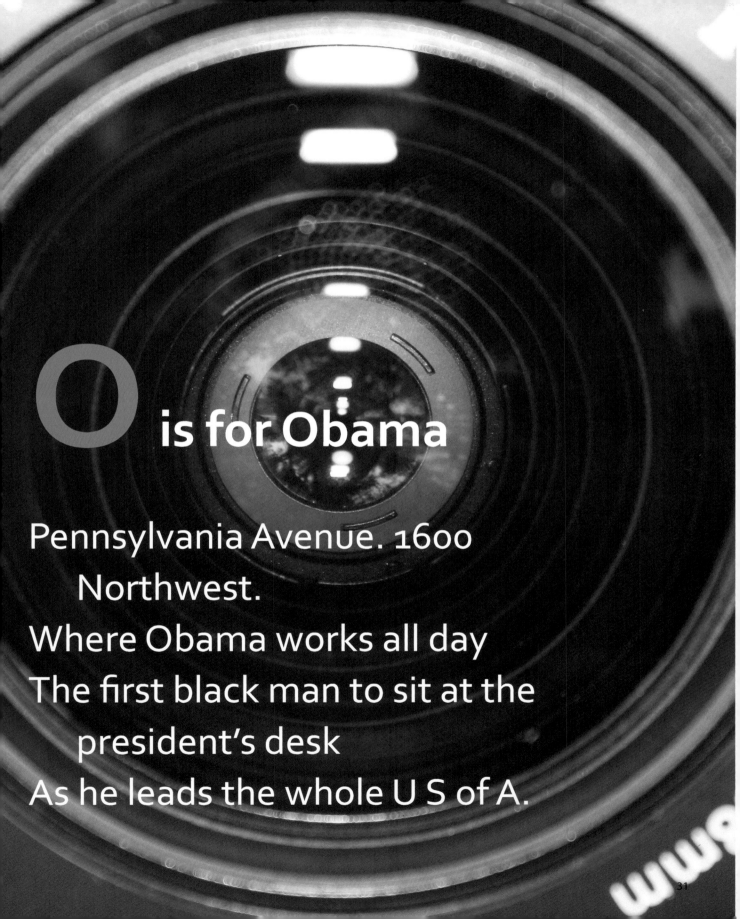

# O is for Obama

Pennsylvania Avenue. 1600
   Northwest.
Where Obama works all day
The first black man to sit at the
   president's desk
As he leads the whole U S of A.

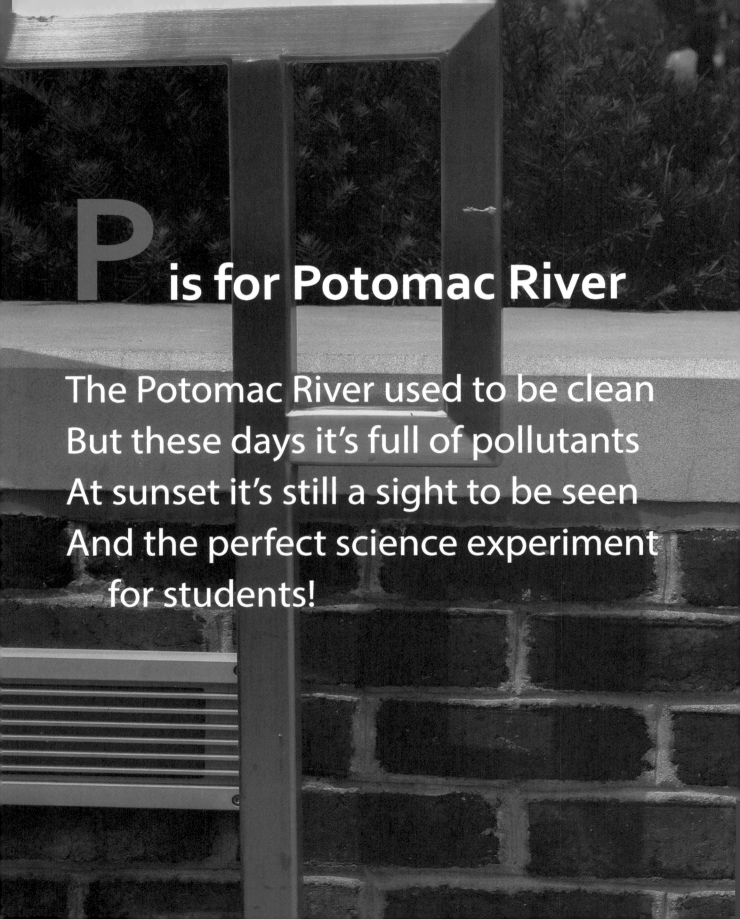

# P is for Potomac River

The Potomac River used to be clean
But these days it's full of pollutants
At sunset it's still a sight to be seen
And the perfect science experiment
    for students!

# Q is for Quadrants

If you just have a number and street
You'll never find that DC address
Without a quadrant, it's incomplete
And you'll get lost and stressed

# R is for Rock Creek Park

Rock Creek – where water you'll find
Nearby you can run or bike
Need time so your mind unwinds?
Take a leisurely nature hike!

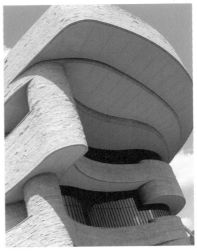

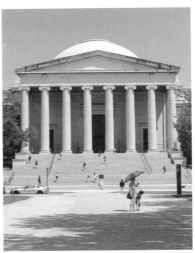

# S is for Smithsonian

When you go downtown for a DC tour
For art or history
The Smithsonian has what you're
   looking for
And best of all, it's free!

# T is for Transportation

Buses, taxis, bikes, and trains
Uptown. Downtown. All around.
Rent Car2Go or take a plane
In DC, many options can be found

# U is for Union Station

Amtrak, Greyhound, or Peter Pan
If you need to get out of the city
You'll find them at Union Station,
  man!
Where you can eat or shop 'til you're
  dizzy

# V is for the Verizon Center

The next stop on our DC tour
Where the red and green lines meet
Whether the Caps' home ice or the
　　Wizards' floor
At the Verizon Center, you'll want a
　　seat

# W is for the Waterfront

At the waterfront in Southwest DC
You can buy fresh fish to eat
Where you're going, you may not see
But you'll smell it from the street

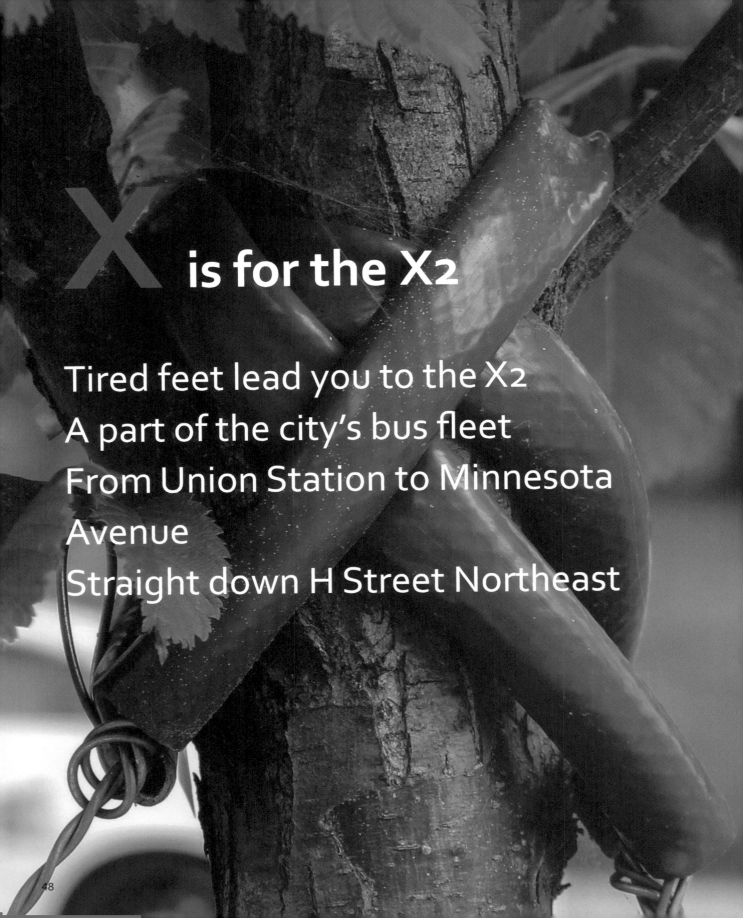

# X is for the X2

Tired feet lead you to the X2
A part of the city's bus fleet
From Union Station to Minnesota Avenue
Straight down H Street Northeast

# Y is for Youth

Y is for us – the city's youth
Authors of this wonderful book
Hope you learned more than you ever
    knew
From our words and the pictures we
    took

# Z is for the National Zoo

We're known for our famous panda
   bears
But we have elephants and tigers too
You can see the lions at rest in their
   lairs
All at the National Zoo

**THE REACH INCORPORATED SHOOTBACK TEAM**
*left to right*: Sean, Fatimah, Arveone, Napresha, Ricardo, Shamya, Neehma, and Marques

**PHOTO CREDITS**
*listed by page number*
**Arveone Harris**: 3, 21, 30, 41
**Fatimah Sumpter**: 4, 8, 11, 15, 17, 18, 22, 25, 26, 37, 41, 53, 55, back cover
**Marques Knight:** 11, 18, 28, 29, 38, 41, 43
**Napresha Parham:** cover, title page, 3, 6, 7, 12, 20, 21, 26, 29, 35, 41, 42, 44, 46, 49, 51, 53, 55, 60
**Neehma Wallace:** 5, 7, 10, 11, 18, 22, 25, 27, 41, 46, 47, 52
**Ricardo Harrell:** 13, 21, 23, 24, 32, 38, 40, 41, 46, 55
**Sean Ross:** 3, 11, 14, 31, 41, 42
**Shamya Whitehead:** 29
**Jonathan Taylor:** 3, 9, 13, 16, 18, 19, 33, 35, 36, 42, 45, 55
**Lana Wong:** 2, 7, 18, 34, 39, 48, 50, 54, 55, 56, 57

### ARVEONE HARRIS

I am in the 10th grade at Ballou Senior High. I enjoyed Shootback because I learned to take pictures of great things. Now, I want to be professional photographer because I love to take pictures. Being a Reach tutor has taught me a lot and is a very important part of my life. It makes me want to go out and do better things. I don't know what I would do if I never joined Reach. My hobbies include cheerleading, basketball, and track. In the future, I want to finish high school, provide for myself, and get a house and a car.

### FATIMAH SUMPTER

I am a 12th grader at Eastern Senior High School. I enjoyed tutoring students with Reach, though sports and other commitments made it hard for me to be as consistent as other tutors. I loved working with Shootback and plan to continue my interest in photography in college next year. I enjoy taking pictures and I'm thinking about making it my career. The project helped me get the real feeling of how it's going to be as a professional photographer.

### MARQUES KNIGHT

I am a 16 year-old student at Ballou Senior High School. Reach was a fun experience for me. It gave me something to do after-school. It also gave me a chance to give back to my community, since I had a tutor once that helped me with my reading. When I'm not at Reach, I like to play video games, play chess, draw, and play basketball. I also like to listen to music, spend time with friends and family, and spend time with my girlfriend. My future plan is to go to MIT and become a technical engineer.

### NAPRESHA PARHAM

I'm a senior at Perry Street Prep. I really enjoyed my three years with Reach and I was proud to become Junior Staff this summer. I'm upset that last year was my last year working with Reach. This summer was really fun. I enjoyed working with the Shootback project and taking photos of DC. During my free time I enjoy writing poetry, talking on the phone, and taking pictures. I plan on going to college next year and am considering studying nursing or social work.

### NEEHMA WALLACE

I'm in 11th grade at Eastern Senior High School. In addition to being a Reach tutor, I'm a singer, dancer, and swimmer...or floater. I love to talk - it's my passion in life. I'm glad I was able to be a part of the Shootback project this summer. We were able to take pictures of DC and the kids will get to read our book this year. When I grow up, I want to go to NC Central and become a psychologist. My goal in life is to be successful!

### RICARDO HARRELL

I tutored for Reach at Perry Street Prep. I enjoyed working for Reach because I was able to spend time with my friends while helping kids become better readers. This summer working with Shootback was a fun experience. I enjoyed taking pictures all over the city. This fall, I'll be in 11th grade at Dunbar Senior High School, and I'm sad they don't have Reach there yet. In my spare time I like to play basketball and video games with my friends.

### SEAN ROSS

I'm a senior at Eastern Senior High School in Washington, DC. My hobbies include spending time with friends and family, playing sports, and eating. As a tutor with Reach, I liked when kids were happy about learning new words or when they improved in reading because of my help. While working with Shootback, I enjoyed taking pictures around DC and learning things about my city. My future plans are to major in engineering, find a good career that I like, and travel.

### SHAMYA WHITEHEAD

I am 16 years old. I go to Ballou Senior High School, and I'm in the 10th grade. My favorite colors are purple, blue, and pink. My favorite thing to do is to take pictures of myself, of course. Working with the Reach program is awesome because we all work together, like this summer. During the school year, I enjoyed working with Reach because we got to know each other and I got to help kids. That's why I signed up to be a tutor again this year.

## ACKNOWLEDGEMENTS

In July 2014, eight students took on a monumental project. Tasked with creating an alphabet book that shares The Real DC, our young people took to the streets with cameras in hand. Using their knowledge, they created an incredible photo book that will educate early readers and engage adults. We are extraordinarily grateful to our photographers and writers for their hard work: Arveone, Fatimah, Marques, Napresha, Neehma, Ricardo, Sean, and Shamya.

We also appreciate the leadership provided by our enthusiastic group leader, Jonathan "JT" Taylor. Jusna Perrin, our Summer Program Director, contributed immensely to keeping the project on time and on track.

We couldn't have done this without our incredible teacher and coach, Shootback founder Lana Wong, who led our teens from the excitement of brainstorming through the editing and selection process. Her talents energized and inspired our novice photographers.

Most of all, we thank those of you who have purchased this book. It is your support that allows us to support teen authors in engaging young readers. We hope the smiles created as you read match those expressed as we wrote the verses and captured the images of our city.

## ABOUT REACH INCORPORATED

Reach Incorporated develops confident grade-level readers and capable leaders by training teens to teach younger students, creating academic benefit for all involved.

Founded in 2009, Reach recruits high school students to be elementary school reading tutors. Elementary school students average 1.5 grade levels of reading growth per year of participation. This growth – equal to that created by highly effective teachers – is created by high school students who average more than two grade levels of growth per year of program participation.

As skilled reading tutors, our teens noticed that the books they read with their students did not reflect their world. We dreamed that our teens could create the books they knew their young students would love. You are currently holding the result of that dream.

By purchasing our books, you support student-led, community-driven efforts to improve educational outcomes in the District of Columbia.

Learn more about all our books at **www.reachincorporated.org/books.**

## ABOUT SHOOTBACK

Shootback empowers young people to tell their own stories and express their creative voices through photography, writing, and critical thinking about the world around them. Founded in Nairobi, Kenya in 1997 by American photographer Lana Wong, Shootback started by putting cameras in the hands of teens in Mathare, one of Africa's largest slums. The project's groundbreaking book *Shootback: Photos by Kids from the Nairobi Slums* was published in 1999 and an exhibition of the Kenyan youths' photographs toured to more than twelve countries around the world. Seventeen years on, Shootback continues to train a new generation of young photographers in Mathare, Shootback alumni have started their own youth photo, film, and media training organizations in the slum, and eight of the original Shootback students are now professional photographers and filmmakers.

In Washington, DC, Shootback is helping to bring photography and writing programs to DC public schools and youth in collaboration with various education nonprofit organizations. Shootback is proud to have partnered with Reach Incorporated on this creative adventure.

Special thanks to DC Public Schools for their support of this collaboration.

**www.shootbackproject.org**

## BOOK EDITING AND DESIGN
Lana Wong

All proceeds from this book will support Reach Incorporated's work in developing confident readers and capable leaders.

JUL 2 7 2015